SYLVIA BRUCE

Essays on Isak Dinesen
and A.E.Housman.

With a tribute to Sylvia Bruce by
Brocard Sewell.

PAUPERS' PRESS.

CONTENTS

Errata:

Two lines have been duplicated at the
bottom of p.16 and top of p.17.
One line has been duplicated at the
bottom of p.20 and top of p.21.

A Tribute to Sylvia Bruce

by

Brocard Sewell.

Sylvia Bruce, who died on 17 June 1993, aged 56, had for much of her adult life to struggle against poverty and ill-health. This held her back from the success and acclaim as a writer that might have been expected to be hers in view of her literary gifts and her enthusiasm for literature.

She was a scholar of Somerville College, Oxford, and graduated MA from the University of London. At Somerville she became a Senior Member. Her interest in the College was lifelong, and she became a close friend of its then principal, Dame Janet Vaughan.

Her first novel, The Powers on High (1964), published in Hutchinson's New Authors series, enjoyed considerable success. Her second, The Wonderful Garden (1969) received high praise from, among other writers, Elizabeth Smart and Henry Williamson. Her poverty at that time was very real, and her state of health far from satisfactory. Her physician certified her as 'unemployable', but the NHS and other statutory bodies were unwilling to accept this, and at one point she was prosecuted for failing to contribute to the National Health Insurance scheme. She chose to defend herself in court, and routed the prosecuting attorney completely. She could have had a brilliant career at the Bar had she so chosen. Her third novel, The Love of a Woman, remains unpublished, but only because of her refusal to change the title, which publishers did not care for.

Sylvia worked for various publishers, and was one of the editors of the Penguin edition of Shakespeare. She was herself a poet and a contributor to the anthology Contemporary Women Poets (1975). In 1987 a selection of her poems, Bemused, was published by The Aylesford Press. At the time of her death she was working on a translation of Eugène Fromentin's novel, Adolphe. As her friend Rosamond Lomax has said: her often difficult life never quenched her passionate and truth-loving spirit.

She was a keen member of The Eighteen-Nineties Society, and had intended to write a biography of Henry Harland; this she gave up when she learned that another writer was at work on a book on the same subject. Another work that she had hoped to achieve was a book on the women pirates.

Sylvia was a firm friend and supporter of the Aylesford Review. Some extracts from her novel The Wonderful Garden appeared, before the book's publication, in the autumn number for 1967 (vol. ix, no.1), preceded by an Author's note, which says : 'We live in a semi-literate society in which it is assumed that everyone who knows the alphabet knows how to read. Few know how to read. Few possess, or ever have possessed, the patience, the

persistence or the humility to submit themselves to the hard task of learning.'
In the same number of the <u>Aylesford Review</u> there is a ten-page review-article by Sylvia on Henry Williamson's novel <u>Lucifer Before Sunrise</u>.
She was a much appreciated presence at the <u>Aylesford Review</u>'s annual literary conferences, held at Spode House, in Staffordshire, and later at Wistaston Hall, Crewe. At the 1992 conference she contributed a paper on Eugène Fromentin's <u>Adolphe</u>. Somewhere I have a photograph of her standing in the hall at Spode House, engaged in conversation with Frances Horovitz and Gabriel Bergonzi : three women of high intelligence and distinguished appearance, whose loss I mourn.

A selection from Sylvia Bruce's critical essays is a decided desideratum. This volume is therefore a welcome sequel to '<u>Dickens's Portrayal of Women</u>' and other essays published by Paupers' Press in 1989 and which included papers on G.K.Chesterton and Virginia Woolf.

SYLVIA BRUCE : 1937-1993.

The Cloak: Isak Dinesen and Seven Gothic Tales

There is a poem, in Ripostes (1912), by Ezra Pound, called 'The Cloak':

> Thou keep'st thy rose-leaf
> Till the rose-time will be over,
> Think'st thou that Death will kiss thee?
> Think'st thou that the Dark House
>   Will find thee such a lover
> As I? Will the new roses miss thee?
>
> Prefer my cloak unto the cloak of dust
>   'Neath which the last year lies,
> For thou shouldst more mistrust
>   Time than my eyes.

This serves as a reminder that when the colour is not specified, we tend to assume that the cloak is black. We speak of the cloak of night. The word 'cloak' comes to us, from Middle English via Old French and medieval Latin, from the same root as cloche: it denotes a loose outer garment, basically rectangular but forming a bell shape, worn by either sex over other clothes. Thus it comes to mean also that which covers over and conceals, a pretext or pretence or outward show.

The Baroness Blixen-Finecke of Rungsted-lund, born, 1885, Karen Dinesen, who, having fallen in love with her cousin Hans, with characteristic perversity and treated per-versely by the Fates (who made her chestnut-haired and killed him), married his twin brother Bror, was much given to pretexts and pretences and disguises, like not a few other

worshippers of truth. '"... Once a thing is
not true," 'says Emilie in 'The Dreaming
Child' (Winter's Tales) ' "it matters little
to me whatever else it may be." ' (page 164).
'Equitare, arcum tendere, veritatem dicere'
reads the epigraph to Out of Africa (1937) -
To ride a horse, to stretch the bowstring, to
speak the truth (or tell the truth) - but
'... my sister couldn't ride or shoot an
arrow, and she never told the truth,' said
Thomas Dinesen, Karen's brother, who won both
the Croix de Guerre and the Victoria Cross.
'You had the feeling that she might suddenly
shoot someone.' When revealed, in 1934, the
year of their publication, as the author of
Seven Gothic Tales, Karen Blixen told an
interviewer from the journal Politiken that
the reason her dead father, Wilhelm Dinesen,
had used a pseudonym ('Boganis') was that 'He
didn't want people to ask, "Do you really
mean that?" Or, "Have you, yourself, exper-
ienced that?" ' Also, as Judith Thurman who
cited this (Isak Dinesen/The Life of Karen
Blixen, George Weidenfeld & Nicolson 1982;
Penguin Books 1984, reprinted 1986, p.86)
says (idem, p. [238], 'To adopt a foreign
language is to mask a prominent and essential
feature of one's identity ...' Isak Dinesen
wrote in English (almost flawlessly) in the
Seven Gothic Tales), sometimes translating,
or rather adapting, into her native Danish
out of dissatisfaction with other people's
renderings, though later she was assisted by
her housekeeper, companion, nurse, the long-
suffering Clara Svendsen. (She herself has
occasional imperfections of idiom, mostly
after the Seven Gothic Tales: 'timber-mare'
may, I think, be 'sawhorse' in Last Tales
[e.g. p.205] and in Winter's Tales [pp. 3,4]
there is 'they were even exactly the

opposite' and 'if worse came to worst'.) To the <u>Politiken</u> interviewer she said 'I moved my own tales back a hundred years to a truly Romantic time when people and their relations were different from now. Only in that way did I become completely free.'* To another interviewer, Daniel Gillès, she said towards the end of her life: '... I have one ambition only: to invent stories, very beautiful stories.'+

That, in <u>Seven Gothic Tales</u>, which I regard as the best of her work, though she herself has other preferences, she incomparably accomplished. Whether the critic Robert Langbaum is correct in stating that she regarded them as 'too elaborate' and too self-revealing I do not know. What <u>is</u> over-elaborate, and therefore artificial, is the sonata form she imposed upon her rather dilettante novel <u>Ehrengard</u>. When she draws attention to her own complexity, her 'second canto' or 'three parts', it is usually a bad sign.

This is what the excellent and still under-rated writer John Davenport said in <u>Twentieth Century</u>, quoted with remarkable good sense on the back cover of <u>Seven Gothic Tales</u> at a time, nearly thirty years ago, when even paperback publishers, some of them, still knew a book from a biscuit, once somebody else had taken it on. Hers, however, had already enjoyed the distinction of being rejected by Faber & Faber.

'Each of the seven tales is as skilfully

---

* Cited Judith Thurman, idem.
+ Op. cit., p. 293

contrived as an interlocking Chinese
puzzle; a ceaseless counterpoint, sharp
as a fugue by Scarlatti; one finds
oneself going through the looking-glass,
or gazing at multiple reflections in
innumerable looking-glasses as each
successive storyteller tells his tale.
The wit burns clear, but it is not cosy
on her heights, where she offers, not
cocoa, but ice and honey dew, in a
crystal air through which may fall a
condor's plume, an eagle's feather;
where the tombs are guarded by live
lions; and the players comport themselves with a noble pride.'

Just as with Brigid Brophy's Foreword to
Elizabeth Smart's <u>By Grand Central Station I
Sat Down and Wept</u>, a later critic is left
with little worthwhile to say. I can at
least give you the titles of the tales. The
order differs in the British and American
editions. The British is that of the original manuscript and that preferred by Isak
Dinesen - who doubtless preferred too her own
version of the titles to those versions
invented by others. Her work began as <u>Nine
Tales by Nozdref's Cook</u> according to Frans
Lasson in his Foreword to the lamentable
posthumous ragbag entitled <u>Carnival</u>, or as
'"Nine Tales also called "Tales of Nozdrev's
Chef" ' according to Judith Thurman, who
mangles, I think, only four titles for the
triumphant seven. These, after authorial
revisions and substitutions, were: 'The Roads
Round Pisa' (not 'Around .. .'), 'The Old
Chevalier', 'The Monkey', 'The Deluge at
Norderney' (not 'Deluge ...'), 'The Supper at
Elsinore' (not 'A Supper ...'), 'The
Dreamers' (plural), and 'The Poet'.

And now the most useful thing I can do is
indicate some of the strands in the web of
Isak Dinesen's cloak. She had other disguises
besides Isak (who, in Hebrew, laughs); she
was, to friends, Tania, for instance, or
Tanne - Widerhall/Letzte Erzählungen, the
German version of Last Tales, titled after
one of the stories within it, 'Echoes'
(Widerhall, or 'sounding again') bears as
author's name Tania Blixen. She had been
'Osceola';* she was 'Pierre Andrézel'; she
was Scheherezade and Pierrot and Ceour de
Lionne, the Lionhearted; she was an aristo-
crat through and through. which allowed her
occasionally to be a peasant; but always
there were certain recognizable fibres. There
was an allegiance to Byron, and a debt to the
great (I am told) Danish poet in whose room
at Rungstedlund she wrote, Johannes Ewald
(1743-1781): she had worn pigtails in tribute
to him, and pigtailed presences occur in her
work. There is, as another massive and tum-
ultuous presence, the cold, crashing sea.
But the strands I have chosen to single out
are those of Norse saga; of Araby or Africa,
with its recurring characters and tales
within tales; and the theatre, including in
her use of it carnival and the commedia del
arte, but particularly Shakespeare. Judith
Thurman points out that numerous 'women
writers' of the nineteenth century began as
the dramatists of their family circle (one
thinks of Jo in Little Women - Jo March).
Isak Dinesen had a foot in more than one

---

* An Indian name, Red Indian, like her
father's pseudonym 'Boganis'.

world and two centuries - her dates are 17
April 1885 to 7 September 1962 - and she was
very modern as well as very old fashioned.
The characters of her Seven Gothic Tales are,
Judith Thurman says with an aptness that
makes one almost forgive the excrutiating
vulgarity elsewhere, 'eighteenth-century
figures adrift in the nineteenth', and 'The
voice which narrates ... is a generation
older than the characters themselves'.* But
behind them is the bluntness of saga and the
sophistication, based on despair, of Scheher-
azade singing not for her supper but her
life.

The story entitled 'The Cloak' is not one
of the Gothic seven, but part of a trilogy
whose other members are 'Night Walk' and 'Of
Hidden Thoughts and of Heaven', out of the
grandiose sequence Albondocani in Last Tales
(which, characteristically, she wanted to
publish before Anecdotes of Destiny).
Albondocani was to have 100 characters and
1,0001 episodes and not surprisingly she did
not complete it. The eponymous cloak is
violet, and embroidered (in brown). There are
precedents in saga for embroidery: both
Hallgerda and Hauskuld have a scarlet cloak
with needlework down to the waist. But the
best cloaks, and the best stories, have no
need of embroidery. As the old coffee-brown,
blackveiled woman in 'The Blank Page' says
(Last Tales, p. 100), 'Where the story-teller
is loyal, eternally and unswervingly loyal to
the story, there, in the end, silence will
speak. Where the story has been betrayed,
silence is but emptiness.' We know where we

---

* Op. cit., p. 292

are when the story-teller Mira Jama, whom we
first meet in 'The Dreamers' but who recurs
in 'The Diver' (<u>Anecdotes of Destiny</u>) says
about Saufe the Softa (Moslem theology
student), 'I myself, when I was a small boy,
have met him in the streets, wrapped in his
shabby black cloak and in a darker cloak of
everlasting loneliness.' It is the world
where silence speaks. ' ... the art of list-
ening to a narrative', says Karen Blixen in
<u>Out of Africa</u> (illustrated edition, p. 173)
'has been lost in Europe. The Natives of
Africa, who cannot read, have still got it.
...' The audience for the saga had it.

To us, saga is strange at first, rebarbat-
ive. Names like Grim, Glum, Swan, Kettle
Rumble, Wolf Squinteye, Thorstein the Un-
stable disconcert, provoking uncertain
reactions. We are not sure we have
understood the intentions. But 'It is not a
bad thing in a tale that you understand only
half of it', the redheaded Lincoln Forsner
remarks to Mira Jama in 'The Dreamers' (<u>Seven
Gothic Tales</u>, p. 243). Saga has a helpful
way of directing you to keep your mind on the
road.

Hogni kept up his friendship with Njal,
and he is now out of the story.

<u>The Story of Burnt Njal</u>, p. 142*

The style is flat, bleak and either incon-
sequential or fatalistic. Such humour as it
has - and there is not much on the subject of
property - is ironical, dour, hardbitten.

* Trans. Sir George Webbe Dasent,
Everyman's Library, 1911

Thiostolf had beaten one of Hauskuld's
house-carles, so he drove him away. He
took his horse and weapons, and said to
Hauskuld,

'Now, I will go away and never come
back.'
'All will be glad at that,' says
Hauskuld.

or:

'What was Njal doing?' she says.
'He was hard at work sitting still,'
they said.
'What were Njal's sons doing?' she
says; 'they think themselves men at
any rate.'

P. 76

and again:

... with that he gave her a slap on the
cheek.
She said she would bear that slap in
mind and repay it if she could.

P. 86

This was the woof to Isak Dinesen's web. In
'The Immortal Story'

The boy [a sailor] stared at her,
immovable except for his broad chest
slowly going up and down with his deep
regular breath. At last he said: 'I
believe that you are the most beautiful
girl in the world.' Virginie then saw
that she had to do with a child.

Anecdotes of Destiny, p. 216

And:

> It was towards the end of our interview
> that she [the narrator's married mistress]
> tried to poison me.
>
> 'The Old Chevalier',
Seven Gothic Tales, p. 59

Intense disapproval of newfangled trends goes
into the comment in 'The Cardinal's First
Tale':

> ' ... this new art and literature - for
> the sake of the individual characters in
> the story, and in order to keep close to
> them and not be afraid - will be ready
> to sacrifice the story itself ...'
>
> Last Tales, p. 23

When that happens:

> ' ... the story itself loses ground and
> weight and in the end evaporates, like
> the bouquet of a noble wine, the bottle
> of which has been left uncorked.'
>
> p. 24

It is the Cardinal speaking.

Brief disposal of anything unconnected
with the story is evident throughout the
sagas; and has its influence. In 'Echoes':

> 'How is it,' she asked, 'that you leave
> the door to your house open when you are
> out and thieves may come in, but that
> you lock it when you are in it yourself?'
> The old man looked at her, then looked

away. 'I do that,' he said.

(This is Pellegrina Leoni the opera singer
and Niccolo the ex-seaman, <u>Last Tales</u>, p.156)

'That was a pity,' said the captain
compassionately. 'Yes,' said Charlie.[*]
'When there is only one person in the
world whom you care for, and that is a
monkey, and he is dead, then that is a
pity.'

'The Young Man with the Carnation',
<u>Winter's Tales</u>, p.14

'And you yourself,' said Charlie
bitterly, 'You go on the errand of a
rich dilettante from one artist to
another. But you have never, upon your
own, painted a picture, or bought one.
When, in time, you quit this world of
ours, you might as well not have lived.'
Æneas [Snell] nodded his head. 'What
do you nod your head at?' asked Charlie.
'At what you are saying,' said Æneas.
'I might as well not have lived.'

'A Consolatory Tale',
<u>Winter's Tales</u>, p.295

A similar comic absurdity occurs in one of

[*] The author or scribe identified
elsewhere as Charles Despard.

the stories in <u>Carnival</u> (p.50):

> At that moment Uncle Théodore [the
> eponym] struck Jacques with his right
> hand a tremendous blow on his left
> cheek and then, contrary to Scripture,
> a second blow on his right cheek. He
> looked as if he wished to continue,
> but as if it were too strenuous for
> him, and after a pause of two or three
> seconds he suddenly sat down again.

The same laconic humour underlies the treat-
ment of Emmanuelson in Karen Blixen's history
of her coffee farm in <u>Out of Africa</u>, who was
based on a wouldbe jack-of-all-trades by the
name of Otto Casparson, as was acknowledged
by Casparson himself.

> 'Do you know anything of book-keeping?'
> I asked him.
> 'No. Nothing at all,' he said, 'I have
> always found it very difficult to add
> two figures together.'
> 'Do you know about cattle at all?' I
> went on. 'Cows?' he asked. 'No, no.
> I am afraid of cows.'
> 'Can you drive a tractor, then?' I
> asked. Here a faint ray of hope
> appeared on his face. 'No,' he said,
> 'but I think that I could learn that.'
> 'Not on my tractor though,' I said,
> 'but tell me, Emmanuelson, what have
> you ever been doing? What are you in
> life?'
> Emmanuelson drew himself up straight.
> 'What am I?' he exclaimed. 'Why, I am
> an actor.'
> ' ... It is a good thing for you,' I
> said, 'that you are not married.'

'Yes,' he said, 'yes.' After a little while he added modestly: 'I am married though.'

Illustrated edition, pp.154-155

Casparson thus connects saga and drama, the real world and theatricals. As he does so, he blurs or dissolves the distinctions, turning the true tragedy of his life into melodrama or farce. Borges, in his essay 'Everything and Nothing' (Labyrinths,* p.284) refers to the 'actor, who on a stage plays at being another before a gathering of people who play at taking him for that other person'. He must not be that other person. The pseudonym 'Isak Dinesen' allows us to pretend we are reading the work of a male. Another author, Olive Schreiner, said 'It is delightful to be a woman; but every man thanks the Lord devoutly that he isn't one' (The Story of an African Farm, Penguin edition, 1971, p. 187), and though through the lips of Lyndall, it was her male persona of Ralph Iron that she said it in. She had, in order to be published, at that time, the early 1880s, to preserve the properties, for men, by using a male identity to say, in an authorial interjection:

Experience teaches us in a millennium what passion teaches us in an hour.

P. 273

For women were not supposed to feel passion.

* Penguin edition, 1970

Still less were they allowed to express views such as those held by Isak Dinesen's Rosendaal the painter:

> 'There was a very nice old woman there [in old Copenhagen], whom I went to see a few times to give her my sympathy and drink a little glass of gin with her, she was seventy-five years old, and blind, and earned her living fairly and honestly by fornication.

Carnival, p. 78

Isak Dinesen, like some other women whom the world chooses to call 'fragile', was stronger than most men. It was with her as with George Sand, of whom Henry James said:

> To feel as Madame Sand felt, ... one had to be, like Madame Sand, a man; which poor Musset was far from being.

'She and He: Recent Documents', The Yellow Book, Volume XII, January 1897, pp. 29-30

So much feeling, so much passion, had to be iced, made formal, distanced, if it was not to seem excessive, absurd, as it often did with George Sand. Even so, passions have consequences, immediate or delayed, congenital or contracted. Whatever her personal history, it was only under a male pseudonym that the Baroness Blixen was able to refer in print to 'the maladies galantes', of which here character Miss Malin Nat-og-Dag (Night and Day), in 'The Deluge at Nordeney' (Seven Gothic Tales, p. 139) 'exhibited a surprising knowledge'. It is to be doubted whether the Baroness's own knowledge came through kissing a statue of St Peter after a sailor had paid his devotions there, as Lady Flora Gordon does in 'The Cardinal's Third Tale' (Last Tales, pp. 97-98). For Miss Malin we are able to offer the excuse that she was happy to be regarded as a little mad; and her creator resembled her in that at least. Does she not almost always make her male characters weaker-willed than the female, even if she remembers to make the males physically stronger - which is by no means always the case in her pages? A weakness (all too sane), in literary terms, is that she gives her males the sympathy towards women which in reality they rarely have unless it is fashionable so to pretend, or which, perversely, women tend to despise them as effeminate for truly having.

Not only may a cloak disguise gender, it may conceal status. In 'Converse at Night in Copenhagen' (Last Tales, p. 318):

> The light from a window for an instant caught the rosy lining of a cloak and caressed a hurrying turquoise-colored silk ribbon; immediately after the street lights glimmered on the braid of a naval officer's uniform which seemed to enclose very round young forms,

and soon we find that we are following, upon similar adventures, 'a very young man, a small frail figure in a large cloak',* who is wandering abroad, as if escaped from the

---

*   Ibid.

Thousand Nights and a Night or Stevenson's
New Arabian Nights, and who is to meet and
drink with the great Danish poet Johannes
Ewald and his harlot mistress. It is the
mad monarch Christian VII of Denmark.
Improbable? But, besides an errant Prince of
Wales or two, there had been other mad
monarchs with a taste for wandering; one
commemorated by Verlaine (whom Isak Dinesen
misquotes) was Ludwig of Bavaria:

When Ludwig was in the country his night
riding had no longer to be bounded by
the four walls of a riding school, and
soon the stories of his midnight excurs-
ions in the valleys of the Bavarian Alps
and into the Tyrol became legendary.
Even in the depths of winter the peasants,
snug in their warm beds, might hear the
bells of his gilded rococo sleigh and
the muffled tread of galloping horses...
rushing past beneath their windows. And
sometimes, when caught in a sudden blizz-
ard, he would seek refuge in a woodman's
hut. The family would hurriedly dress,
logs would be piled on the stove and
beer brought, while the King chatted
easily with his host; he was never shy
or silent in the company of simple
people. Then, the storm abating, he
would wrap himself up again in his huge
fur coat, pick up the broad-brimmed hat
with its sparkling diamond clasp and
vanish once more into the night. And a
few days later some inappropriate gift,
such as a great bunch of lilies from
the hot-houses at Nymphenburg, would be
delivered in gratitude for hospitality
received - tangible proof that the royal
visit had after all been a reality and

not a dream.

Wilfred Blunt,
The Dream King/Ludwig II of Bavaria,
Penguin Books, 1973, p. 160

On one occasion Ludwig gave a shepherd boy a silver watch*

I must not forget to establish the Gothic credentials of these tales. Ewald's cloak 'had once been black, but now after many years of service showed shades of green and gray' (Last Tales, p. 340); the Virgin's cloak is as usual ultramarine; neither of these is what we mean by Gothic.
In 'Carnival' the mode is satirized:

'That is very charming' said Julius,
'the black and brimstone sky, and a
ruin to the left, and in the middle
distance a Polish horseman in a
scarlet cloak, galloping under the
ancient curse of his family, who die
when they make love.'

Carnival, p. 77

The Rex Whistler cover of Seven Gothic Tales, in sepia and faintest rose, depicts horse and becloaked, batlike rider with heads bowed against the wind and the gathering storm as they attempt, amid all but leafless trees, a precipitous zigzag ascent past a gorge with tumbling waterfall, toward, it may be, an

* P.170
embattled tower, like any Childe Roland. And we have, within, not only all the paraphern-

embattled tower, like any Childe Roland. And
we have, within, not only all the paraphern-
alia that make, in lesser hands, the Gothic
so tedious and unintentionally so comical to
many readers - the bones, chains, pistols,
werewolves, deliquescent flesh, portraits,
chests, cabinets, cellars, and the true story
solemnly but unconvincingly sworn to - but
also such a passage as this:

> At a place where the road got steeper,
> through the mist of the loose whirling
> snow which was driven along the ground
> like the smoke from a cannon, I [Lincoln
> Forsner] caught sight of a dark shadow
> in front of me, not a hundred yards away,
> which might be a human figure. At first
> it seemed to disappear and to appear
> again, and it was difficult in the night
> and in the storm to keep your eyes fixed
> upon it. But after a time, although I
> got no nearer, my eyes became used to
> their task, and I could follow her
> steadily. She [Olalla, alias Rosalba,
> alias Pellegrina Leoni] walked, on this
> steep and heavy road, as quickly as I
> myself did, and my old fancy about her,
> that she could fly if she would, came
> back. The wind whirled her clothes
> about. Sometimes it filled them and
> stretched them out, so that she looked
> like an angry owl on a branch, her
> wings spread out. At other times it
> screwed them up all around her, so that
> on her long legs she was like a crane
> when it runs along the ground to catch
> the wind and get on the wing.

> 'The Dreamers',
> <u>Seven Gothic Tales</u>, pp. 277-78

(It has not been mentioned in this extract that she was wearing a cloak, but she was, and I hope you received the impression that she was.)

Isak Dinesen says somewhere that there has to be a little charlatanry in art, by which I take it that she means or includes a little sleight of hand. Her own sometimes took the form of an aristocratic disdain for accuracy; which may be creative. Thus in the epigraph to one of the chapters in her preposterous novel <u>The Angelic Avengers</u> - and it has to be said that a novel, or, like the slight, graceful, yet diffuse and vapid <u>Ehrengard</u>, a novella approaching novel length, is not the form to which her talents are best suited - her pleasure-dome, unlike Coleridge's, is not 'stately' but 'mighty'; which makes it fortunate that it is only concerning a quotation from <u>Hamlet</u> that her character Zosine in the same work asks Lucan, and the reader, 'Is it right?' Her recitation is, or very nearly, and she knows it is. Isak Dinesen knows her Shakespeare backwards and forwards, like a lover - well enough to take the accepted liberties with him that one great artist may occasionally do with another. 'All my life I have held that you can class people according to how they may be imagined behaving to King Lear,' she says in <u>Out of Africa</u> (p. 279). In 'Tempests', the story in <u>Anecdotes of Destiny</u> which was her tribute to John Gielgud after seeing his Hamlet at Kronborg Castle, and his Prospero, and hearing him read, the song 'Full fathom five' suffers a sea change, for she transposes its original second, third and first person to first person entire. Unfamiliarity with Danish Bibles makes me not too sure of the significance of the fact that in the same

work one in a bourgeois household is open at
the twenty-ninth chapter of Ecclesiasticus -
the Apocrypha - but I insist that it is sheer
artistic license that accounts for the
following, in 'The Old Chevalier':

> I thought what a strange thing is a
> young man who runs about, within the
> selfsame night, driven by the mad
> passion and loss of two women.
> Mercutio's words to Romeo about it
> came into my mind, and, as if I had
> been shown a brilliant caricature of
> myself or of all young men, I laughed.

> Seven Gothic Tales, p. 72

Now, you will search in vain for any such
speech of Mercutio's , for he does not make
it. It is possible that the allusion is to
Benvolio's words beginning 'Tut, man, one
fire burns out another's burning' (I.2.45),
more probable that it is to Friar Laurence's

> Holy Saint Francis! What a change is
> here!
> Is Rosaline, that thou didst love so
> dear,
> So soon forsaken?

> II.3.60-63

Mercutio dies apparently unaware that Romeo
has fallen in love with a member of the house
of the hated Capulets. His quarrel is with
Tybalt, who also does not know. But Isak
Dinesen had no need, for her own artistic
purposes, of a name that would evoke saint-
liness, or gravity, or even good intentions.

She needed no shadowy friar, or friend offer-
ing sage spurned counsel, whose name we
forget to look up in the cast list unless he
has grossly overplayed his part. She needed
quicksilvery youth - so she conjured it up.
Her legerdemain did not always involve other
authors. There is the conjuring trick whereby, in 'The Cardinal's First Tale', the lady
in black cries out 'for the third time', 'As
I myself!',* when her first such exclamation
had occurred only two paragraphs before, and
was not repeated - by the University of
Chicago Press at least, perhaps entering into
the spirit of the thing. Similarly we are
given the Cardinal's third tale but no
second. Perhaps she did not write it.
Perhaps we are being encouraged to adopt a
sceptical and a questioning disposition. Or
is it to combat such a disposition that, in
his third tale, the Cardinal exclaims of Lady
Flora Gordon:

> 'And surely the woman who sets her pride
> in denying all, will find help with him
> who, before the cock crew the third time,
> three times had denied!' +

Yet in the Gospels cockcrow is never triple.
In Matthew XXVI it is 'Before the cock crow,
thou shalt deny me thrice'; Mark XIV has
' ... before the cock crow twice'; Luke XXII
'I tell thee, Peter, the cock shall not crow
this day, before that thou shalt thrice deny
that thou knowest me'; and John XII 'Verily,
verily, I say unto thee, the cock shall not

---

* Last Tales, p. 4.
+ Op. cit., p.90.
crow, till thou hast denied me thrice.' It

crow, till thou hast denied me thrice.' It
is a little unkind, if deliberate, to attrib-
ute such an egregious error to a prince of
the Church. Most of the ecclesiastics in
Isak Dinesen are bizarre; less so than in
Firbank, admittedly. It is not their tastes
that are unusual, but their experience.
Bizarre things befall them.

She was arbitrary. She could be cruel and
capricious. But then, abnormal demands were
made on her. As she herself says in 'The
Diver' (<u>Anecdotes of Destiny</u>) 'pearls are
like poets' tales: disease turned into love-
liness' * Others would have compared not the
pearl to the story, but the story to the
pearl. It was like her to invert.

Her conception of pity and mercy and horror
probably owed more to Shakespeare than
to Aristotle or the Scriptures. Among modern
writers, though there are resemblances with
Sylvia Townsend Warner and with Carson
McCullers (who gave a dinner party for her
at which the other guests were Marilyn Monroe
and Arthur Miller), she is closer still to
Djuna Barnes. The despairing rhetorical
question of Pellegrina Leoni in 'Echoes':

> 'Why must pity of human beings,' she
> asked herself, as again she chased
> away the picture [of Lincoln Forsner,
> her sometime lover], forever suck the
> marrow from my bones?'

> <u>Last Tales</u>, p. 163, repeated
> in different form p. 189

* P. 12.

is one that the transvestite doctor in
Nightwood agonisedly and continually asks;
and the spinechilling reversals of sex, in
'The Roads around Pisa', which shock afresh,
as they are meant to, at each fresh reading,
achieve the same grue (to use the Scots word)
- that *frisson* which characterises the highest art and for which there is so far as I am
aware no word in English. Such a world, in
either writer, is not camp in the least,
despite in 'The Roads Round Pisa' the powder
and the paint, the crossdressing, the scarlet
mouth; for these are a convention, like
greasepaint in the theatre, and the characters are on stage. Their actions are acts,
their acts are actions. Both works Nightwood
and Seven Gothic Tales, are misunderstood by
those who do not know, or will not accept,
the difference between perversity and
perversion. It is not, perhaps, incidental
that Karen Blixen (like her friend and Finch
Hatton's friend Berkeley Cole) had the red
hair shared according to legend by Christ and
Judas and Cain. It arouses antagonism in
people, and by some that antagonism is
returned. Charles Despard says to Æneas
Snell in 'A Consolatory Tale' (Winter's
Tales, p. 291):

' ... All human relationships have in
them something monstrous and cruel.
But the relation of the artist to the
public is amongst the most monstrous.
Yes, it is as terrible as marriage.'

And again (p. 292):

'We cannot show mercy to one another.
The public cannot be merciful to an
artist: if it were merciful it would

not be the public. Thank God for
that, in any case. Neither can an
artist be merciful to his public, or
it has, at least, never been tried.'

Isak Dinesen does appear to make, though
mockingly, a plea for mercy from the public
in her epigraph to <u>The Angelic Avengers</u>: it
is a self-quotation from a later page (110)
of that work:

> <u>You serious people must not be too hard</u>
> <u>on human beings for what they choose to</u>
> <u>amuse themselves with when they are shut</u>
> <u>up as in a prison, and are not even</u>
> <u>allowed to say that they are prisoners.</u>
> <u>If I do not soon get a little bit of fun,</u>
> <u>I shall die.</u>

But she has herself provided the case for
the prosecution, and her friend Denys Finch
Hatton's haunting quotation is also relevant:

> You must turn your mournful ditty
> To a merry measure
> I will never come for pity
> I will come for pleasure.

Besides, in <u>Shadows of the Grass</u> (1960), the
appendage to <u>Out of Africa</u>, she sabotages the
case for the defence:

> For my own part, in order to save my
> reason [at the outbreak of the Second
> World War], I had recourse to the remedy
> which, for that same purpose, I had used
> in Africa in times of drought: I wrote a
> novel ... and - since I looked upon it
> as a highly illegitimate child - it was

published under the pseudonym of Pierre Andrézel.

Pp. 114-15

In disowning it and fathering it elsewhere, she had reckoned without paperback publishers: hers have blazoned it forth as by, all in capitals, ISAK DINESEN/(KAREN BLIXEN)/ AUTHOR OF/<u>OUT OF AFRICA</u> ('acclaimed the most breathtakingly romantic film of the decade').
The novel <u>The Angelic Avengers</u> is reminiscent, it appears, to the blurbs department, of, somehow, Emily Brontë <u>and</u> Jane Austen. It is enormously enjoyable, as if by a more vigorous <u>Branwell</u> Brontë out of Daphne du Maurier or Lady Eleanor Smith (<u>The Man in Grey</u>) with Jean Rhys as midwife and occasional appearances by Daisy Ashford:

Mr. Tabbernor from time to time laid
his cigar on a flower pot to applaud
a particularly graceful figure.

Penguin Books, 1986, p. [45]

The dialogue and exposition attain almost inimitable heights of stiltedness:

Mr. Penhallow for a moment stared at
him, and then smilingly replied, 'So
this is really you, Noël? No, I beg
your pardon,' he corrected himself.
'Sir Noël. I am already aware of the
change of your fortunes. Your cousin
has died from a fall from his horse,
and you are now Sir Noël Hartranft.
But what brings you to France, Noël?'

P. 117

There is an outsize, unhinged and devoted West Indian called Olympia. There are pale, quivering lips, faces as white as chalk, and the author allows her characters to let their hands pass over their eyes. There are unctuous villains. In the garden is a shambling brute called Clon, and even if the blurb had not dropped heavy hints, the introduction of the white slave trade would not have come as a surprise. It _is_ a surprise, however, that in the closing pages we have what seems like a guest appearance by Barbara Cartland:

> Lucan wondered whether she ought to
> tell her husband of what had happened
> to her at Fairhill, and whether she
> ought perhaps to have done so a long
> time ago. Could he blame her because
> a man had dared to make her an offer
> like Mr. Armworthy's? But if she told
> him of it, she thought, he would fire
> up in a dangerous way ... She had been
> in charge of a treasure. It belonged
> to Noël, it was his by right, and had
> been so from the beginning of things,
> and she would have died rather than
> ever to fail or betray him ... She had
> brushed her pretty hair, and hidden it
> in her bonnets, because it was his.

Pp. 302-303

Not merely is the morality offered utterly shallow and debased, the sentiments of a prostitute with the soul of a parlourmaid, but aesthetically the author offends, in this work and other of the inferior pieces, by explaining too much. The answer to the question 'Why?' should rarely be supplied

in fiction.* But anybody who does not com-
prehend why universities which still retain
pretensions to intellectual or aesthetic
rigour cannot admit Gone With the Wind to
their courses in English Literature (I do not
speak of their History courses) will undoubt-
edly feel the same about the exclusion of The
Angelic Avengers.

Why should it not be admitted to the canon?
It is writing, after all, just as graffiti
are, and literature is writing. Here I fall
back upon a disclaimer of Isak Dinesen's own,
in 'Tempests' (Anecdotes of Destiny, p. 97):

> ... a poet cannot be expected to have
> an insight both into versifying and
> his points of the compass.

Whether or not Isak Dinesen knew a hawk from
a handsaw, or handsel from herons, she knew,
I think, a nor'nor'easter when she encount-
ered it, yet she would probably have rated
versifying higher than seamanship, or at
least than sailing; and she knew that Elsinore is flat, but she knew too, as well as
Shakespeare did, that more biting truth
whereby the action of Hamlet has to take
place on a cliff. Literature is about the
higher truth. And as the Jewish clerk Elisha
tells Virginie, of easy not to say symp-
athetic virtue in 'The Immortal Story', the
one every sailor tells, 'In this pattern the
road runs the other way. And runs on.'
(Anecdotes of Destiny), p. 191)

Many of the personages in the tales of Isak
Dinesen are wayferers, metaphorically or

* Detective fiction apart

actually.   In 'A Country Tale' (<u>Last   Tales</u>,
p. 238) there is Eitel:

> As he made this decision [to visit a
> condemned prisoner he had known] he
> felt like a man who, having lost his
> way in woods and moors, comes upon a
> road.   He knows not whereto it leads,
> whether to salvation or destruction,
> but he follows it because it is a
> road.

Sometimes it seems like a road into, or part
of, a picture, and that picture, Paradise:

> The afternoon was so perfectly still,
> so golden, that he felt as if he had
> found his way into a picture, some
> classic Italian painting, that suited
> him well.

This is Axel in 'The Invincible Slave-Owners'
(<u>Winter's   Tales</u>, p. 139); the   cultured and
cosmopolitan Herr Cazotte in <u>Ehrengard</u> is
more detailed, more informed, as he writes
his   letter to her who was the   great grand-
mother of the old lady who narrates (p. 31):

> <u>Imagine to yourself that you be quietly</u>
> <u>stepping into a painting by Claude</u>
> <u>Lorraine, and that the landscape around</u>
> <u>you becomes alive, balsamic breezes</u>
> <u>wafting and violets turning the mountain</u>
> <u>sides into long gentle waves of blue</u>

At the beginning of 'The Roads Round Pisa'
(<u>Seven Gothic Tales</u>, p. 9)

> He [the Danish traveller Count Augustus
> von Schimmelmann] took a small object

>from his waistcoat pocket and looked at
it. It was a smelling-bottle, such as
ladies of an earlier generation had been
wont to use, made in the shape of a
heart. It had painted on it a landscape
with large trees and a bridge across a
river. In the background, on a high hill
or rock, was a pink castle with a tower,
and on a ribbon below it all was written
'Amitié sincère'.

And

>Perhaps, he thought, some day I shall
come across the bridge under the trees
and see the rock and the castle before
me.
>
>   P. 10

For him, as well as for the becloaked boy he
meets, who says it, 'time was like a road
through a pleasant landscape on which I could
wander to and fro as I fancied' (p.   22).
Near the end, after his wanderings and
strange adventures, he is brought back to the
beginning:

>... she [his new acquaintance the old
Countess di Gampocorta] took from her
pocket a small object and handed it to
him.
>   Augustus looked at it, and unconsciously
his hand went up to his breast. It was
a small smelling-bottle in the shape of
a heart. On it was painted a landscape
with trees, and in the background a white
house. As he gazed at it he realized
that the house was his own place in
Denmark. He recognized the high roof
of Lindenburg, even the two old oaks in

front of the gate, and the long line of
the lime-tree avenue behind the house.
The stone seat under the oaks had been
painted with great care. Underneath, on
a painted ribbon, were the words 'Amitié
sincère'.

P. 50

But this is not quite the end, not quite the
beginning. The beginning and the end, for him
and for the reader, will be a new adventure,
quest, ordeal or examination - an examination
of the self in a new light.

Augustus took a small mirror from his
pocket. Holding it in the flat of his
hand, he looked thoughtfully into it.

P. [51]

When we look into mirrors, we do not see what
we expected to see.

THE CONTENTS OF THE DRAWER

W.H. Auden's sonnet 'A.E. Housman' is not, one feels and hopes, the poem by which its author would have most wished to be remembered. Nevertheless he chose to include it in his Collected Shorter Poems 1927-1957, and it may have already formed for some their first idea of Housman. Mr Kingsley Amis (as he then was) has said that it 'enabled a whole generation to feel superior to one who had never bothered to hide his own, perhaps justified, feelings of superiority' (Sunday Telegraph, 26 June 1988).

No one, not even Cambridge, was to blame
(Blame if you like the human situation):
Heart-injured in North London, he became
The Latin Scholar of his generation.

Deliberately he chose the dry-as-dust,
Kept tears like dirty postcards in a
drawer;
Food was his public love, his private
lust
Something to do with violence and the
poor.

In savage foot-notes on unjust editions
He timidly attacked the life he led,
And put the money of his feelings on

The uncritical relations of the dead,
Where only geographical divisions
Parted the coarse hanged soldier from
the don.

Collected Shorter Poems 1927-1957,
Faber and Faber mcmlxvi, page 126

That is one view of him, snobbish and
sneering. He is, we are to believe, a pedant
who made the mistake not only of having,
which is rather sentimental, a heart, but of
allowing injuries to it to occur in North
London. He is not only a Latin scholar but
the Latin scholar in flippant capitals. He
is, the tone suggests, a glutton. His
motives for being interested in justice are
questionable. His concept of justice is con-
fused. He speculates with his feelings; and
his sense of lacrimae rerum, his sorrow for
the human condition, is hoarded away furtive-
ly for the rare occasion when he can bring it
out in order to share an equally furtive
snigger, presumably with someone else from
Cambridge - or North London.

Here is another view; to one of a generation that shared Houseman's own reticence
(Ifor Evans in his Short History of English
Literature) he was 'a classical scholar of
the highest order, seemingly a remote and
authoritative personality, yet sensitive in
one friendship to an extent that affected his
whole life.' (Penguin Books, 1940; 3rd edition 1970, reprint of 1971, p.110).

Then there is the view of the parodists. I
will not quote Max Beerbohm (who did not like
Housman), because he usually has a keener ear
for prose than for verse, and he seems to me
to fail to catch Housman's distinguishing
manner, but here is Humbert Wolfe, himself a
poet, though an uneven one:

A.E. Housman

When lads have done with labor
    in Shropshire, one will cry,
"Let's go and kill a neighbor,"
    and t'other answers "Aye!"

So this one kills his cousins,
   and that one kills his dad;
and, as they hang by dozens
   at Ludlow, lad by lad,

each of them one-and-twenty,
   all of them murderers,
the hangman mutters: "Plenty
   even for Housman's verse".

Parodies/An Anthology from Chaucer
to Beerbohm - and After,
ed. Dwight Macdonald, Faber and
Faber mcmlxi, p. 209

   Housman's own favourite among the parodies
is unfaithful in one feature only, the
inclusion of a foodstuff. There is plenty of
drink, but apart from one mention of breakfast, one of poisoned meat, one of 'Company
and beef and ale', and the stanza

   'Long for me the rick will wait,
     And long will wait the fold,
   And long will stand the empty plate
     And dinner will be cold',

(A Shropshire Lad VIII)

I can find no mention of food, or foods, for
human beings in serious verse by Housman.
The poem 'Loveliest of Trees' contemplates
the cherry's blossom, not its fruit; in the
translation from Horace of the 'Diffugere
nives' (The snows have fled) it is only
incidentally that 'Comes autumn, with his
apples scattering', and 'Blithe the girls go
milking' only as background to 'God's Acre';
the only grapes are the grapes of the anger
of God in 'The Defeated', and 'The Olive', in

the poem of that title, is symbolic of endur-
ance. Nor is there a hearty breakfast for
the condemned man so prominent in Housman's
work, whether he swings in chains or awaits
his last, early-morning, eight o'clock; which
is rather odd for the gourmand suggested by
Auden. Housman was a gourmet, particularly
fond of saddle of hare. One hotelier named a
dish after him, and he made his own salad,
both in restaurants and in college, but he
always ate in moderation.

Here is the Shropshire Lad as depicted by
Hugh Kingsmill:

What, still alive at twenty-two
A clean upstanding lad like you?
Sure, if your throat tis hard to slit,
Slit your girl's, and swing for it.

Like enough, you won't be glad,
When they come to hang you, lad:
But bacon's not the only thing
That's cured by hanging from a string.

So, when the spilt ink of the night
Spreads o'er the blotting pad of light,
Lads whose job is still to do
Shall whet their knives, and think of
    you.

Parodies, ed. Macdonald, p. 210

Unlike Jack Worthing in The Importance of
being Earnest, Housman was not a Shropshire
lad, and only part of the poetry in the cycle
has to do with his imagined Shropshire, which
bears much the same relation to reality as
Hardy's Wessex, or on a lower level Winifred
Holtby's South Riding or Arnold Bennett's
Five Towns. According to F.C. Horwood, to

whose <u>A.E. Housman/Poetry and Prose: A Sel-
ection</u> (Hutchinson, 1971) I am indebted for
some of the biographical information throughout,* Housman was born in Worcestershire, at
Fockbury, in 1859, a solicitor's son, and his
family moved the next year to Bromsgrove in
the same county; it was there that he went to
school. He won a scholarship to St John's
College, Oxford, to read Classics (Moderat-
ions, or Mods, and Greats as it is called
there), for part of the time sharing lodgings
in St Giles' with the historian A.W. Pollard
and the scientist Moses Jackson, who was to
have a very great influence on his life. His
two fellow lodgers both took a first class
degree; Housman gained a First in Mods - and
failed Greats, leaving Oxford without a degree. Eleven years later, 1892, he became
Professor of Latin at University College,
London (of which Moses Jackson had been a
graduate), his application supported by many
scholars. In the interim he had taken a Pass
degree, taught at his old school, Bromsgrove,
and prepared for Civil Service examinations,
joining his great friend Moses Jackson, al-
beit in a more lowly capacity, at the Patent
Office in 1882, to work during the day as a
clerk. In the evenings he read Latin and
Greek literature in the British Museum,
mainly studying Propertius. From 1882, the
year his first scholarly publication, a paper

---

* The biography by Richard Perceval Graves,
  <u>A.E. Housman/The Scholar - Poet</u> (Routledge
  and Kegan Paul, 1979, O.U.P. edn 1981),
  though useful, is disfigured by an inabil-
  ity to distinguish between poetry and
  autobiography: conjectures are treated as
  facts.

on Horace, appeared, to 1886 he shared lodgings in the Bayswater Road with Moses Jackson and Jackson's younger brother Adalbert. He then removed to Byron Cottage, Highgate (Auden's 'North London', presumably). The following year, Moses Jackson went out to India and Housman was then to live alone for nineteen years. When Jackson married, Housman eventually became godfather to one of the four sons. Adalbert the younger brother died in 1889 (there is a poem dedicated to A.J.J.), and Housman's own youngest brother (he had four younger brothers and two sisters) was killed in action during the Boer War. A Shropshire Lad appeared in 1896, Housman's translation of the Astronomica of Manilius from 1903 onwards (dedicated to M.J.J.),* his Juvenal in 1905. In 1911 he was made Professor of Latin at Cambridge. No testimonials were required of him. He was awarded a Fellowship at Trinity College, Cambridge, and an Honorary Fellowship at his old college, St John's, Oxford. The Last Poems, an infelicitous title, appeared in 1922, a year before the death of Moses Jackson, who was by that time in Vancouver. Housman's edition of Lucan followed in 1926, his Leslie Stephen lecture at Cambridge The Name and Nature of Poetry in 1933, the posthumous More Poems in 1936 and Additional Poems in the Collected Poems of 1939. He had refused the award of the Order of Merit in 1929, and he refused numerous honorary degrees. It was assumed he would refuse also the office of Poet Laureate. He did not like his poems to be anthologized, or read on the wireless. His ashes are buried at Ludlow,

* The initials of Moses John Jackson

outside the parish church.

Far from worshipping the dry-as-dust, Housman responded physically to the literature that attracted him. In a well-known passage in <u>The Name and Nature of Poetry</u> he describes how 'Experience has taught me, when I am shaving of a morning, to keep watch over my thoughts, because if a line of poetry strays into my memory, my skin bristles so that the razor refuses to act.'

But besides being a sensual man, a poet and a scholar, Housman was a man of common sense. His Introductory Lecture of 1892 as Professor of Latin at University College, London, is to be commended to all those who have been led astray by the doctrine of 'relevance' in education, which has led first to our having too many engineers and next too few scientists - pure scientists.

'The partisans of Science', he says, 'define the aim of learning to be utility [the old name for relevance]. I do not mean to say that any eminent man of science commits to this opinion: some of them have publicly and scornfully repudiated it, and all of them, I imagine, reject it in their hearts. But there is no denying that this is the view which makes Science popular; this is the impression under which the British merchant or manufacturer dies and leaves his money to endow scientific education. ... The popular view, I say, is that the aim of acquiring knowledge is to equip one's self for the business of life; that accordingly the knowledge most to be sought after is the knowledge which equips one best; and that this knowledge is Science [as we would now say, applied science, or engineering]. ... Our business here is not to live, but to live happily. We may seem to be occupied, as Mr Spencer [Herbert Spencer] says, in the production, preparation and distribution of commodities; but our true occupation is to manufacture from the raw material of life the fabric of happiness; and if we are ever to set about our work we must make up our minds to risk something.'

Housman risked his life on several occasions, one of them including the rescue of a woman who had climbed too high; and he risked or sacrificed his money in addition to his feelings. A Shropshire Lad was not the original title of his first book of poems. He had to be dissuaded by his historian friend A.W. Pollard from calling them Poems by Terence Hearsay. (Terence, it will be remembered, was a great comic writer. No.LXII of A Shropshire Lad begins with the self-addressed 'Terence, this is stupid stuff'; it ends with the disclaimer ' - I tell the tale that I heard told./Mithridates, he died old.') Macmillan rejected this volume; it was published at Housman's own expense by Kegan Paul. The second edition was brought out by that amiable rogue Grant Richards (twice bankrupt). The work has never been out of print since the year of its first publication. Housman declined to receive royalties on it, literature not being his trade, he said - the implication being that literature is not a trade at all.

A Shropshire Lad was appreciated by Edith Nesbit among others; she sent a copy to W.E. Henley (whose own verse Housman despised). He found it 'very monotonous' (Katherine Lyon Mix, A Study in Yellow: The Yellow Book and its contributors, University of Kansas Press, Lawrence, and Constable, London, 1960, p.132) Francis Thompson, more discerningly, found it 'monotonous, but not wearying'. It is for the most part single-toned, which may even be its attraction for composers. Thompson also found it 'grim, strong, close-knit, commanding attention by its virile pessimism' (The Academy, 8 October 1898, cited G. Krishnamurti, compiler, The Eighteen-Nineties/ A Literary Exhibition, National Book League, 1973, p.88) What sometimes tends not to be seen is that Housman was a wit. It was certainly not accepted by his brother Laurence. Laurence - like most other contributors to The Yellow Book - was rather a rum cove: well known as an an illustrator and later a dramatist, but also the anonymous author of An English-woman's Love Letters (John Murray, 1900). The brothers were not entirely devoted, though fond. Alfred was in general a dutiful and generous son and brother, but told Laurence 'I had far far rather have my poems mistaken as yours, than your poems mistaken as mine.' (Laurence Housman, The Unexpected Years, Indianapolis, 1936, p. 137, cited K.L. Mix, p. 270). In Laurence's My Brother A.E. Housman (London, 1938, p. 174, cited K.L.Mix, p. 17) Alfred is quoted as saying about female suffrage 'I think I should like to see some other and less precious country try it first: America for instance. ...' (Laurence, on the other hand, was one of Mrs Pankhurst's converts.)

Alfred Housman was by no means incapable of writing parody himself. All the features of the classical drama which have put generations of schoolchildren and some undergraduates off that form are admirably captured in his 'Fragment of a Greek Tragedy' rich in the compound adjectives of which he makes more serious use elsewhere. I quote the first four lines of the opening Chorus:

O suitably-attired-in-leather boots
Head of a traveller, wherefore seeking
   whom
Whence by what way how purposed art
   thou come
To this well-nightingaled vicinity? ...

He was an intensely literary writer. The
influences upon his work that he recognized
were the songs of Shakespeare (he was espec-
ially fond of the Dirge from <u>Cymbeline</u>), the
Border ballads, by which is meant here their
Lowland Scots versions, and Heinrich Heine,
but in English there is also the Bible and
the Book of Common Prayer, there is Michael
Drayton, there are Andrew Marvell and other
Metaphysicals, and in No.XLVI of <u>A Shropshire
Lad</u> there can be felt not only the same
spirit that moves in Feste's second song
in <u>Twelfth Night</u>; a speech of Ophelia's
and Gertrude's lament for her; and lines
from <u>Othello</u>; but also several poems of
Wordsworth's; Milton's <u>Lycidas</u>; and anonymous
medieval lyrics.

Bring, in this timeless grave to throw,
No cypress, sombre on the snow;
Snap not from the bitter yew
His leaves that live December through;
Break no rosemary, bright with rime
And sparkling to the cruel clime;
Nor plod the winter land to look
For willows in the icy brook
To cast them leafless round him: bring
No spray that ever buds in spring.

But if the Christmas field has kept
Awns the last gleaner overstept,
Or shrivelled flax, whose flower is blue
A single season, never two;

Or if one haulm whose year is o'er
Shivers on the upland frore,
 - Oh, bring from hill and stream and
   plain
Whatever will not flower again,
To give him comfort: he and those
Shall bide eternal bedfellows
Where low upon the couch he lies
Whence he never shall arise.

The Collected Poems of A.E. Housman,
Jonathon Cape, 1939; paperback edn 1967,
reprint of 1986, pp. 50-51

That is a comparatively indifferent poem: the
influences lie somewhat too heavily upon it
and too near the surface; the debt is repaid,
but not the interest. I do feel, however,
that when Housman has been accused of self-
parody, usually he has been deliberately
parodying the ballads. Of one poem, XXIII in
Last Poems, I can only say that either it is
quite a good parody of a lesser ballad or it
is a shocking bad poem. The common reader
has had no difficulty in appreciating Housman
and knows doggerel when he meets it. To fail
to recognize the humorous is a privilege of
journalists and on occasion a difficulty of
dons.

> In the morning, in the morning
> In the happy field of hay,
> Oh they looked at one another
> By the light of day.
>
> In the blue and silver morning
> On the haycock as they lay,
> Oh they looked at one another
> And they looked away.

Collected Poems, p. 88

Housman's response to another ironist, Heine, included an adaptation of his eight-lined poem "Am Kreuzweg wird begraben" from Traumbilder (Dream Pictures) in the Junge Leiden 1817-1821 (Youthful Sufferings), collected in Buch der Lieder (Songbook). I give first a free rendering in verse of my own, then the Heine, then what Housman makes of it (five quatrains).

At the crossroads lies buried
The man who did himself in.
There grows a flower, blue,
For the poor fellow's sin.
At the crossroads I stood and sighed;
Cold and mute was the night.
Hangdog in the moonlight
Moved, slow, the flower of rue.

Am Kreuzweg wird begraben
Wir selber sich brachte um;
Dort wächst eine blaue Blume
Die Armesünderblum.
Am Kreuzweg stand ich und seufzte;
Die Nacht war kalt und stumm.
Im Mondschein bewegte sich langsam
Die Armesünderblum.

Buch der Lieder LXII, Insel Verlag, Frankfurt, 1981, p. 101

It is noteworthy that Housman does not here include the sighing so familiar in his own verse, and the moonlight is implicit.

SINNER'S RUE

I walked alone and thinking,
    And faint the nightwind blew
And stirred on mounds at crossways
    The flower of sinner's rue

Where the roads part they bury
    Him that his own hand slays,
And so the weed of sorrow
    Springs at the four cross ways.

By night I plucked it hueless
    When morning broke 'twas blue:
Blue at my breast I fastened
    The flower of sinner's rue.

It seemed a herb of healing,
    A balsam and a sign,
Flower of a heart whose trouble
    Must have been worse than mine.

Dead clay that did me kindness,
    I can do none to you,
But only wear the breastknot
    The flower of sinner's rue.
            [the wild chicory]

Last Poems XXX, in
Collected Poems, p. 93

An example of a debt repaid with interest
is No. XL of A Shropshire Lad. Housman draws
upon two ballads, 'Thomas the Rhymer' and
'The Dæmon-Lover'. Three stanzas from
'Thomas the Rhymer':

'O see ye not yon narrow road,
    So thick beset with thorns and briers?

That is the path of righteousness,
    Though after it but few enquires.

'And see ye not that braid braid road,
    That lies across that lily leven?
That is the path of wickedness,
    Though some call it the road to heaven.

'And see not ye that bonny road,
    That winds about the fernie brae?
That is the road to fair Elfland,
    Where thou and I this night maun gae.'

> Border Ballads, ed. William Beattie,
> Penguin Books, 1952, reprint of 1965,
> p. 224

A stanza from 'The Dæmon-Lover':

'O what hills are yon, yon pleasant hills,
    That the sun shines sweetly on?'
'O yon are the hills of heaven,' he said,
    'Where you will never win.'

> Border Ballads, p. 194

Housman's poem in all its poignancy:

Into my heart an air that kills
    From yon far country blows:
What are those blue remembered hills,
    What spires, what farms are those?

That is the land of lost content,
    I see it shining plain,
The happy highways where I went
    And cannot come again.

> Collected Poems, p. 43

There beats behind Housman's verse the drum
of the ballad of four centuries. He takes
from the ballad his grammatical framework and
his rhythms, his sometimes archaic diction,
he takes the starkness of outlook, the harsh,
murderous world of treachery and betrayal and
occasional rare loyalty to the one irreplace-
able love. There are two main differences,
one of them leading to some artificiality:
the lack of the background (like a Western's)
of cattle-rustling (reiving). The other is
that whereas in the traditional ballad the
responsibility or blame for infidelity is
divided equally between the sexes, in Housman
the seducer, attempted or actual, is always
the male, often of his best friend's girl who
is merely a party to crime or sin which the
poet regards stoically as a fact of life.

His own especial contribution to prosody is
usually regarded as being the five-line
stanza, of the four-line ballad metre rhyming
usually abab, plus an extra line rhyming with
its predecessor. The first poem in which he
uses this doublet (<u>A Shropshire Lad</u> VII),
however, 'When smoke stood up from Ludlow',
has a main unit not the four-foot line of
eight syllables but a line of six syllables
with seven as variant. I think it possible
that it was the blackbird's alarm call, with
its repetition 'chink-chink', that suggested
his verse's doubling and the internal repetition.

    The blackbird in the coppice
       Looked out to see me stride,
   And hearkened as I whistled
      The trampling team beside,
     And fluted and replied:

> 'Lie down, lie down, young yeoman;
>   What use to rise and rise?
> Rise man a thousand mornings
>   Yet down at last he lies,
>   And then the man is wise.'

Collected Poems, p. 15

For if Housman was deeply literary, he was also steeped in country lore. He knows the missel-thrush as the storm-cock, the butter-cup as the goldcup, the daffodil as the Lent or Lenten lily. His is an England in which darnel still grew not only in wasteland, as in Walter de la Mare's poem 'Nicholas Nye', but also, with other rye-grasses, in arable land, like charlock. He knows and mentions many trees, among them the aspen with its 'rainy-sounding silver leaves' (A Shropshire Lad, XXVI). Argent again is the palm in No.X ('March') - not of course the date-palm but the sallow willow with its silvery female flowers and lance-shaped leaves.

> Afield for palms the girls repair,
> And sure enough the palms are there,
> And each will find by hedge or pond
> Her waving silver-tufted wand.

Collected Poems, p. 19

But he is at his best in describing not individual trees but a whole forest, as in the poem which has been set by several composers, has given the title of a novel to Patrick White (The Tree of Man) and perhaps influenced that of Henry Williamson's The Gale of the World. Uricon is the Roman camp of Uriconium or Viriconium, now known as

Wrexeter.

A Shropshire Lad, XXXI

On Wenlock Edge the wood's in trouble;
    His forest fleece the Wrekin heaves;
The gale, it plies the saplings double,
    And thick on Severn snow the leaves.

'Twould blow like this through holt and
    hanger
    When Uricon the city stood:
'Tis the old wind in the old anger,
    But then it threshed another wood.

Then, 'twas before my time, the Roman
    At yonder heaving hill would stare:
The blood that warms an English yeoman,
    The thoughts that hurt him, they were
    there.

There, like the wind through woods in
    riot,
    Through him the gale of life blew high;
The tree of man was never quiet:
    Then 'twas the Roman, now 'tis I.

The gale, it plies the saplings double,
    It blows so hard, 'twill soon be gone:
To-day the Roman and his trouble
    Are ashes under Uricon.

                    Collected Poems, p. 36

There are few writers - one thinks of
Arthur Machen - who have as acute sense of
history under foot. It is the same with

astronomy. Housman had a profound interest
in the subject - hence his translation of
Manilius - but again it is not the poems
which give the greatest detail from myth or
actuality about the planets which are most
effective, but those where he uses his grasp
of their identities and movements to give a
feeling of the rotation of our globe and all
the poor devils confined to it.

<u>Last Poems</u>, XX

The night is freezing fast,
    To-morrow comes December;
        And winterfalls of old
Are with me from the past;
    And chiefly I remember
        How Dick would hate the cold.

Fall, winter, fall; for he,
    Prompt hand and headpiece clever,
        Has woven a winter robe,
And made of earth and sea
    His overcoat for ever,
        And wears the turning globe.

<u>Collected Poems</u>, pp. 86-87

For he did think we were all poor devils,
If there was confusion in his thought, it was
the confusion of the atheist, originally a
deist, whose mother had died, on his birth-
day, when he was twelve, who finds the
universe deplorable and can find nobody to
blame for it, nor anyone to swear to or by
when he needs to. In the words of a poem
from which the title of my own first novel
was taken,

A Shropshire Lad, XXXIII

If truth in hearts that perish
　　Could move the powers on high,
I think the love I bear you
　　Should make you not to die. ...

Collected Poems, p. 37

Another poem that appealed to me greatly when
I began writing that novel, The Powers On
High, at the age of 18 was one which some
have called, with apparently pejorative
intent, 'adolescent'; they say the same thing
about Byron.

Last Poems, XII

　　The laws of God, the laws of man,
He may keept that will and can;
Not I: let God and man decree
Laws for themselves and not for me;
And if my ways are not as theirs
Let them mind their own affairs.
Their deeds I judge and much condemn,
Yet when did I make laws for them?
Please yourselves, say I, and they
Need only look the other way.
But no, they will not; they must still
Wrest their neighbour to their will,
And make me dance as they desire
With jail and gallows and hell-fire.
And how am I to face the odds
Of man's bedevilment and God's?
I, a stranger and afraid
In a world I never made.
They will be master, right or wrong;
Though both are foolish, both are
　　strong.

And since, my soul, we cannot fly
To Saturn nor to Mercury,
Keep we must, if keep we can,
These foreign laws of God and man.

<u>Collected Poems</u>, p. 79

There is a text in Isaiah (LV.8) which reads 'For my thoughts are not your thoughts, neither are your ways my ways, saith the Lord.' Housman was fond of giving his own twist to a Biblical verse. Thus whereas the reading of Isaiah LV.1 is 'Ho, every one that thirsteth, come ye to the waters, and he that hath no money; come ye, buy, and eat ...', Housman says (<u>More Poems</u>, XXII)

Ho, everyone that thirsteth
   And hath the price to give,
Come to the stolen waters,
   Drink and your soul shall live. ...

<u>Collected Poems</u>, p. 123

He had learned from Proverbs IX.17 that 'Stolen waters are sweet, and bread eaten in secret is pleasant.'

In rather a mysterious poem (<u>More Poems</u>, XXVIII), the allusion is not, I think, to Pilate's washing of his hands in the Gospel according to St Matthew, but Coverdale's translation of Psalm XXVI.6: 'I will wash my hands in innocency, O Lord: and so will I go to thine altar'.

He, standing hushed a pace or two apart,
   Among the bluebells of the listless
     plain,
Thinks, and remembers how he cleansed
   his heart
And washed his hands in innocence in
   vain.

Collected Poems, p. 126

Above all, perhaps, Housman is the soldier's poet, the poet who understands the conflict of loyalties, fear, desertion - desertion either of one's family, friends, lovers or of one's country. The war sometimes belongs to Roman, Saxon or Celtic times, sometimes to Victorian. Sometimes, as here, the participant, perhaps on both sides, is a laughing cavalier.

More Poems, XXXVII

I did not lose my heart in summer's even,
   When roses to the moonrise burst apart:
When plumes were under heel and lead was
   flying,
   In blood and smoke and flame I lost my
   heart.

I lost it to a soldier and a foeman,
   A chap that did not kill me, but he
   tried;
That took the sabre straight and took it
   striking
   And laughed and kissed his hand to me
   and died.

Collected Poems, pp. 131-2

When Housman says, in <u>More Poems</u> XLVI,

> ... Oh, said I, my friend and lover
>   take we now that ship and sail
> Outward in the ebb of hues and
>   steer upon the sunset trail ...

the words 'my friend and lover' are quite clearly addressed to a male. There is no fudging the issue; there is no indecency either. Housman commiserated with the sufferings of Oscar Wilde; after Wilde's discharge from prison he sent him a copy of <u>A Shropshire Lad</u>. Although Wilde had been immured in Holloway,* Wandsworth and Reading gaols, not Portland, there is in the Additional Poems (XVIII) one which has a close bearing upon his case and the indignities inflicted on him:

> O who is that young sinner with the
>   handcuffs on his wrists?
> And what has he been after that they
>   groan and shake their fists?
> And wherefore is he wearing such a
>   conscience-stricken air?
> Oh they're taking him to prison for
>   the colour of his hair.
>
> 'Tis a shame to human nature, such a
>   head of hair as his;
> In the good old time 'twas hanging
>   for the colour that it is;

---

* As Housman's sister Clemence the wood-engraver and novelist was to be for her feminist activities

Though hanging isn't bad enough and
   flaying would be fair
For the nameless and abominable colour
   of his hair.

Oh a deal of pains he's taken and a
   pretty price he's paid
To hide his poll and dye it of a
   mentionable shade;
But they've pulled the beggar's hat
   off for the world to see and stare,
And they're haling him to justice
   for the colour of his hair.

Now 'tis oakum for his fingers and the
   treadmill for his feet
And the quarry-gang on Portland in the
   cold and in the heat,
And between his spells of labour in
   the time he has to spare
He can curse the God that made him for
   the colour of his hair.

                    Collected Poems, pp. 152-3

How little justice there is in Auden's
caustic reference to Housman's

                    '... private lust
   Something to do with violence and
   the poor'

may be seen when it is set against Last Poems
XXXVII,

EPITAPH ON AN ARMY OF MERCENARIES

These, in the day when heaven was falling,
  The hour when earth's foundations fled,
Followed their mercenary calling
  And took their wages and are dead.

Their shoulders held the sky suspended;
  They stood, and earth's foundations stay;
What God abandoned, these defended,
  And saved the sum of things for pay.

Collected Poems, p. 101

A poet has to be judged, however, not by his sense of justice but his poetry. As Housman himself put it in The Name and Nature of Poetry, 'Poetry is not the thing said but a way of saying it.' It is often a way of saying one thing while appearing to say something different, perhaps the opposite: thus in the poem 'White in the Moon' a strong impression is given of gusts and moving shadows though stillness is asserted. I made some use of this poem in the opening chapter of my novel The Powers On High to show the schoolgirl protagonist experiencing the onset of a nervous breakdown; the lines present themselves to her in a distorted form (White-in-the-lune, the wrong road lies ...). In a subsequent chapter the sentence 'Headlights, dipping as they turned the corner, chased elongated, flitting shadows down the road and pavements' is only in part indebted to what we laughingly call 'reality', much more to the impressions given me by this poem, A Shropshire Lad XXXVI. Influence can be, and often is, oblique.

White in the moon the long road lies,
    The moon stands blank above;
White in the moon the long road lies
    That leads me from my love.

Still hangs the hedge without a gust,
    Still, still the shadows stay:
My feet upon the moonlit dust
    Pursue the ceaseless way.

The world is round, so travellers tell,
    And straight though reach the track,
Trudge on, trudge on, 'twill all be well,
    The way will guide one back.

But ere the circle homeward hies
    Far, far must it remove:
White in the moon the long road lies
    That leads me from my love.

Collected Poems, p. 40

My favourite amongst all Housman's work comes from More Poems (VI). I would not presume to differ from Professor Christopher Ricks over the merits, real or imagined, of Mr Bob Dylan, but I do differ from him if, as F.C. Horwood says, he regards the rhythm here as a blithe contrast with the meaning. I find it to be an ominous and fitting expression of that meaning, which is beyond paraphrase.

I to my perils
    Of cheat and charmer
    Came clad in armour
        By stars benign.
Hope lies to mortals
    And most believe her,
    But man's deceiver
        Was never mine.

The thoughts of others
    Were light and fleeting,
    Of lovers' meeting
        Or luck or fame.
Mine were of trouble,
    And mine were steady,
    So I was ready
        When trouble came.

Collected Poems, pp. 114-15

It is by such a poem that I prefer to
remember Housman. Auden - who was equipped
to have understood Housman better - I would
remember by his lullaby that begins

Lay your sleeping head, my love,
Human on my faithless arm.

Paupers' Press : a checklist of available titles:

BLYTHE, Daniel : The Good, the Bad and the Ugly : moral ambiguity in the Tales of the Brothers Grimm. £5.50. Paper. 30pp. 0-946650-45-4.

BRINER, Patricia and WISE, Peter : Marking Time : conversations across a kitchen table. £5.95. Paper. 70pp. 0-946650-39-X.

BRUCE, Sylvia : 'Dickens's portrayal of women' and other essays. £4.95. Paper. 45pp. 0-946650-13-6.

BRUCE, Sylvia : Essays on Isak Dinesen and A.E.Housman (with a tribute to Sylvia Bruce by Brocard Sewell). Price not set. Paper. c.60pp. 0-946650-55-1.

DALGLEISH, Tim : The Guerilla Philosopher : Colin Wilson and Existentialism [Colin Wilson Studies, no.5] £5.95/£13.95 Paper/Hardback. 40pp. 0-946650-47-0 Paper 0-946650-48-9 Hardback*

LACHMAN, Gary : Two essays on Colin Wilson : World Rejection and Criminal Romantics & From Outsider to Post-Tragic Man. [Colin Wilson Studies, no.6] £7.95/£15.95 Paper/Hardback. 64pp. 0-946650-52-7 Paper 0-946650-53-5 Hardback*

LAWS, Robert Anthony : Dance of the Hanging Men : the story of Francois Villon; killer, thief and poet. £11.95. Paper. 107pp 0-946650-50-0

MCQUARRIE, Bruce (ed.) : A book about MacQuarries featuring 'The MacQuarrie Heritage' by Rodney L. McQuary, B.D.,D.D. £9.95. Paper. 104pp 0-946650-18-7.

MOORHOUSE, John : A Historical Glossary of British Marxism. £4.95. Paper. 48pp. 0-946650-06-3.

MOORHOUSE, John and NEWMAN, Paul : Colin Wilson, two essays : 'The English Existentialist' and 'Spiders and Outsiders' (including an interview with the author.) Edited by Colin Stanley. [Colin Wilson Studies - vol.1] £4.95/£12.95 Paper/Hardback. 50pp. 0-946650-11-X.Paper 0-946650-36-5 Hardback*

POWER, David : David Lindsay's Vision (with an introduction by Colin Wilson) £5.95/£13.95. Paper/Hardback. 40pp. 0-946650-30-6 Paper 0-946650-31-4 Hardback*

ROBERTS, Paul : Becoming Mr. Nobody : the philosophy and poetry of John Cowper Powys.
£6.95/£14.95. Paper/Hardback. 54pp. 0-946650-37-3 Paper 0-946650-38-1 Hardback*

SEWELL, Brocard : Three essays (including the original introduction to Colin Wilson's 'Voyage to a Beginning'). [The Aylesford Review Essays - v.1.]
£4.95. Paper. 24pp. 0-946650-07-1

SMALLDON, Jeffrey : Human Nature Stained : Colin Wilson and the existential study of modern murder.
[Colin Wilson Studies - vol.4.]
£4.95/£12.95. Paper/Hardback. 38pp. 0-946650-28-4 Paper
0-946650-29-2 Hardback.*

STANLEY, Colin : The 'Aylesford Review', 1955-1968 : an index.
£5.50. Paper.. 89pp. 0-946650-03-9.

STANLEY, Colin : 'The Nature of Freedom' and other essays.
[Colin Wilson Studies - vol.2.]
£4.95/£12.95. Paper/Hardback. 33pp. 0-946650-17-9 Paper
0-946650-27-6 Hardback.*

TREDELL, Nicolas : Caute's Confrontations : a study of the novels of David Caute.
£11.95. Paper.. 124pp. 0-946650-51-9

TREDELL, Nicolas : Uncancelled Challenge : the work of Raymond Williams.
£8.95./£15.95. Paper/Hardback 96pp. 0-946650-16-0 Paper
0-946650-46-2 Hardback.*

TROWELL, Michael : Colin Wilson, the positive approach: a response to a critic.[Colin Wilson Studies - volume 3.]
£4.95/£12.95. Paper/Hardback. 36pp. 0-946650-25-X Paper
0-946650-26-8 Hardback.*

vanVOGT, A.E. : A Report on the Violent Male (with an introductory note by Colin Wilson).
£5.95/£13.95. Paper/Hardback. 36pp. 0-946650-40-3 Paper
0-946650-41-1 Hardback.*

VINCENT, Gregory K. : Proportional Representation : a debate on the pitfalls of our electoral system.
Price not set. Paper. c26pp. 0-946650-54-3.

WADE, Stephen : More on the Word-Hoard : the work of Seamus Heaney. £11.95. Paper. 132pp. 0-946650-49-7

WADE, Stephen : No Secondary Themes : essays on the poetry of Peter Russell, Stanley Burnshaw, Peter Dale, Stevie Smith and Idris Davies. £6.95. Paper. 68pp. 0-946650-42-X

WILLIAMSON, Henry : 'Some notes on 'The Flax of Dream'...' and other essays.[The Aylesford Review Essays - volume 2].
£4.95/£12.95. Paper/Hardback. 32pp. 0-946650-10-1 Paper
0-946650-19-5 Hardback.*

WILSON, Colin : Autobiographical Reflections
£4.95/£12.95. Paper/Hardback. 50pp. 0-946650-09-8 Paper.
0-946650-20-9 Hardback.*